Letters of a Long Name

poems by

Ginger Hanchey

Finishing Line Press
Georgetown, Kentucky

Letters of a Long Name

Copyright © 2019 by Ginger Hanchey
ISBN 978-1-63534-921-4 First Edition
All rights reserved under International and Pan-American Copyright Conventions. No part of this book may be reproduced in any manner whatsoever without written permission from the publisher, except in the case of brief quotations embodied in critical articles and reviews.

ACKNOWLEDGMENTS

I would like to thank the editors of the following journals where these poems, sometimes in different forms, first appeared:

Dunes Review: "How to Explain" and "Symphony"
Foundry: "Milk"
Into the Void: "Epiphany"
Nashville Review: "Visiting the Memory Care Ward"
Rust + Moth: "Letting Down: 3 Years After the NICU"
San Pedro River Review: "Fall"
Snapdragon: "Round Top in March"
Tar River Poetry: "Be Mine" and "Wound"
Whale Road Review: "On the Brazos"

"Lake Bolsena, Italy" was a finalist in the 2019 *Atticus Review* poetry contest.

Publisher: Leah Maines
Editor: Christen Kincaid
Cover Art and Design: Cassidy Trier
Author Photo: Alex Engebretson

Printed in the USA on acid-free paper.
Order online: www.finishinglinepress.com
also available on amazon.com

Author inquiries and mail orders:
Finishing Line Press
P. O. Box 1626
Georgetown, Kentucky 40324
U. S. A.

Table of Contents

I.
How to Explain 1
Babybook 2
Be Mine 3
Fall 4
At the Children's Hospital 5
Epiphany 6
Dinner on the Way out of Town 7
Before and After 8
Good Friday Poem 9

II.
Halftime 12
Picture Day 13
Milk 14
Wound 15
On the Brazos 17
Lake Bolsena, Italy 18

III.
Winter Visit 20
Voyeur 21
Visiting the Memory Care Ward 22
Gianicolo, Rome 23
Letting Down: 3 Years after the NICU 24
Round Top in March 25
Symphony 27
Hospital Wall Art 28

For Dan

…everything that touches us, me and you,
Takes us together like a violin's bow…
Upon what instrument are we two spanned?
And what musician holds us in his hand?
Oh sweetest song.
—RILKE, *translated by Stephen Mitchell*

And the sons we get to have, our light, Oliver and Atticus.

I.

How to Explain

A children's hospital has to be learned
through immersion. What could compare?
When I left town to be with him
and came home again to my other little boy,

the dead stalks of flowers were cleared away
by friends, even their snow of detritus,
little fallen parts of themselves,
vacuumed clean.

How could they know I needed them?
In Fort Worth I slept in an apartment
sprung up new like a crop.
At the end of everyday (of dying?

of mending?) I could stand at the window,
look across a field with a tiny glittering skyline
at the end, hanging from my neck like a jewel.
It was a skyline, a field, and me, alone.

What things do we try to make beautiful?
The memorial outside his window cast names
in shadow: sunlight moved through inkless words
etched on glass, left giant renderings

on rock behind it. John Ryan Gage, age 3 ¾.
The distance between the etching
and the rock. The distance between the three-fourths
and the four.

Great fields of absence everywhere.

Babybook

Everywhere I looked for
a book of you
to tell your story,
but there were no blanks
for the emptiness
that happened to us.
Only prompts of
Joy! Triumph! Progress!
Nothing that let me say
how I felt on the day they shaved
your head, soft black hairs shorn
before I could even hold you.

Be Mine

At the hospital where
he was born, I watched
babies float home
like petals on water.

My hands smelled like perfume
for months, thorn pricked
from washing. Later,
the children's hospital

issued us containers to collect
the time: a laundry basket, space
on a kitchen cabinet, shelves
of a deep freeze for milk. Old

memories rode in on winter.
Once, my mother nursed
a tiny fallen bird in our kitchen,
its cardboard box a bed

and then a coffin. I didn't
know how to stop crying.
Every time I offered him
my finger, he wrapped his

hand around it and
we were more true than God
almost touching Adam. But
even so I could not

feed him. It seemed like
he was a stone sent skipping
across a large body of water,
so much distance to the other

shore. Gravity, his mother.

Fall

Minutes, hours exist outside
the NICU, but here life is measured
in other ways: by ounces gained
or lost, by the leaking out

of proteins, white blood cells,
hope. On days when
I leave him to work, I pass
through a door where a white

bird has fallen. I can't help
but look into its hollow place,
watch feathers shelter its growing
emptiness. Here, my lullabies

are naked. Machines spin their webs
of neon sound. From the window
I look to a vast parking lot, then a freeway,
and further still fields that are fallow

now with fall. Leaves whip everywhere,
cut from invisible trees that are nowhere.
They perform their frenetic dance
like embers around a fire, rend

something inside me.
I wish I could lift the glass, know the wind
on my face again,
watch it animate the one behind me,

twirl him madly about in so many
breathtaking directions, let him
dance just a bit
before the winter finally falls.

At the Children's Hospital

Do it to Julia
The man said on
The last page of *1984*,
Suffering whatever it was
That was his greatest
Fear. In this place
If I had to choose
Between science and God
I would choose
Science every time,
The prayers, meditations,
Rejoicing of my life
But the preliminary,
The equivalent only of
Front matter.

Epiphany

When I woke in the night,
saw the stars suffocating
in heavy blackness, I prayed
again my wordless, dry-heave
of a prayer for him to live
but there was no echo, no
bottom to the well where
my coin would land and
sound back up hope.
There was no God,
only this bottom of a well
and the fathomless space
up above, crushing,
smothering me.

Dinner on the Way out of Town

Everywhere, concrete.
Clouds, half-breaths
against the sky. You
move the car and I
hate you the way
an animal hates
an animal who hates
it back, our little
son, no longer the horizon
we look to,
strapped in silence
behind us. This,
like everything else,
new: language
of the body, painful
bouts of milk-surge,
roads to the place
where he lies
100 miles from here.
Outside, the ground cracks
like a broken windshield,
like ice smeared over
with tar. Me, always
hungry, everything always
tasting like ash.

Before and After

My baby wastes in a breadbox, hungry
and unable to eat.

            Outside his room
a mural spans the wall: a family,
a kitchen, white chef hats atop happy
faces, powder white flouring their air,
an egg, with its cool, hard
symmetry held in suspense
above a bowl.

To see it is like walking into a room
and not remembering
why. What does this have to do
with me, I wonder. What
does any of this have to do with me?

Good Friday Poem

I.

When Moses' people needed water,
desert-thirsty masses, he lifted the
staff in his hands, touched the rock with it, rock
split open with floods. Enough for the people,
even enough for their beasts.

II.

Pilate needs water to clean the political
mess off his hands, standing off from the filth
of the masses who crave Christ's blood
on them, Christ's blood even on their
children. Pilate pushes Christ into
other hands, who press a staff into Christ's
own hand. Did his fingers wrap around it
instinctively, like a babe in a cradle
grasps the parental finger? Hail the pitiful
king! Shame somehow held in his
palm, encircled by his own skin and bone.

Later, Christ needs water from the Cross,
but doesn't get any. Tastes the wine and gall,
closes his mouth again. I wish he could
want it, could take it, could have some small
comfort before his body finally splits
in two, water pouring from his side. No
father, no comfort. Like swollen, bursting
fruit, the voice that was silent before
Pilate now spills out in pain.

The curtain splits, also, like the Red Sea
parting, providing safe passage to God.
But who is there now in the dark, to go
through it? And who is the God that waits
silently on the other side?

Little to do now, except bury hope
and him together. So many Josephs.
This one, rich, of the leaders but not
of them, offers clean rock to receive
the body, muddies his reputation at
the moment he could have begun
to rebuild it, rejoin the victors.

Seal it all up with stone, this beauty.
These gifts of love. Let us wander
the deserts again.

II.

Halftime
> *Or, On Bringing My First Son Home from the Hospital
> Two Days after His Full-Term Birth*

You are the armful of roses
and I am—finally—
the queen of homecomings.

Picture Day

Toward the end of the year
I found in a drawer
A packet of my oldest son's school
Pictures. What day was this?
I had never seen them, did not
Know they were happening,
Wondered who had dressed him,
Knew I had not brushed

His hair. His eyes
Looked at me from so many
Frames, haunting
Iterations of all the days
Of him I had missed.

Milk

He lived on IV fluids for months.
Even the smallest trace of milk
caused him to vomit blood. They
told me to keep pumping, how good
it would be for his system if he could
ever tolerate food. And in this distorted
dream-world, I let it be my mother-love
(the grief and the milk both in endless supply),
a way to express something even if
the pots of ink were white.

I didn't see it until later, like in a dream
that unfolds after waking, but you were there
doing this: taking the bottles of milk in the night
when I pumped them, or in the day, pouring them
off into meal-apportioned bottles—so careful not
to spill—and with black ink registering
the day and the hour of our love,
so that now, when I stand at the freezer,
I see row after row of our duet of prayer and elegy
stored against the day when he would live.

Wound

I try to avoid a place
on his side
when I bathe
him or lift him bare-chested

at the pool, where my hand
would slip in
through the ribs,
folds of skin deep and concealing

its closure. Gaps in memory,
real as hair
falling out,
spot the early years with him,

how we spent the second
Christmas,
for instance.
I mostly choose not to look

at pictures. I have heard sufferers
say anorexia
pushes them
past mirrors. Like an egg sliding from its shell

they fall past them. But what would they
see if they turned
to look in? Here.
Let me go back to his six-month-old

self, slide my hands
underneath his slight
body, turn them
and splay my fingers

as I lift him up
to me. Then, my chin to his head,
breathe him in slowly. Hold him
like I know

he is going
to live.

On the Brazos

By the river my brother was named for,
my two sons jump from rock to rock,
big one loping in front of the small one.

I nearly lost them both:
one to a failing body,
the other to the grief that almost overwhelmed me.
They are my two miracles,
like the gift of the river, and the gift of the land.
The younger one jumps wildly and the rock catches him every time.
The older one tires, comes up beside me, puts arms around my waist.
Happiness spreads beneath my skin like a bruise.

Lake Bolsena, Italy

The water, there is so much of it. Once we tried to walk around the rim, traced maybe 5%. When his brother was born, stitched into a hospital, we said, *Here is what to do with fear: reach into the water, fold the soap into, around your hands, let the water run.* But he is years beyond this now, has added new rituals—rich, lustrous blooms around the crater. This morning his brother pulled rocks from the lake, found emerald glass, but quickly dropped it. You can hold it, we said. The water takes away its edges. See? You can turn it over in your hand.

III.

Winter Visit

He turns eleven today and I try
to name my sadness: He is the night we
climbed eighty steps in Switzerland while
my sister, tired and newly single, stayed

at home to cook. We followed Andy's steps,
unlikely Sherpa, small nephew uprooted
and upwards-hiking, to his overlook
and met the night more quickly with our climb.

Cold Babylon! Blue panoramic view
starred everywhere with ice. Expanse of life
before us stinging lonely in our chests.
And us, tongue stuck for telling how the beauty

seemed so tragic; painful puffs of breath-
shrouds closed around. I looked beside me, wondered
who could bench themselves and face the frozen fountain,
thought: How precarious the way back down.

Voyeur

From behind me at the flea market
a woman makes a shushing sound—
shock when I see the knot on her
grown son's back. He can't drop
the melody he sings. Under her breath
she tells him to look around, see the other
people, they have to be quieter. I
calculate when to turn again, send my
silent message as a smile, but the mother
and the handsome brother, too, both
practiced in imperviousness, leave it behind
them with all the other trinkets they don't want
to buy, make their way to the next room. I
reach for the rim of a plate, the word
BOSTON emblazoned in blue on its
center.

———

To have the boys he wants as friends come
to our house would be embarrassing. He
tries to explain why. Something to do with
how we care for him.

———

At the end of the day, my younger son
and I wait in the dark for sleep to come,
a compact of silence between us.
We watch his arm lean toward the wall
like a stem toward light, small hand dipping
and flittering atop it. I try to think what
he must be imagining, his hand alighting
on air with the movements of a sparrow
in nearby branches before it darts away
into some veiled, unwatched beyond.

Visiting the Memory Care Ward

My grandmother said   he only ever cried once,
when his mother died,   briefly as a light
rain even then.   Today I don't think
he knows me until he   tucks his chin to his chest
and weeps,   says he wants
to go home.   He drinks
cranberry juice   from a styrofoam cup
and my 3-year-old   watches him
delightedly,   drinks when he drinks.
In the far corner   a woman lies
on a ration   of sunshine,
big body curled up confident,   cat-like.
Another approaches,   berates us
with profane words,   exhorts us
back to work.   My grandmother
says she once managed   an airplane
production line,   implies there was something
in the metal,   seeds of dementia.
When my mother   was growing up,
my grandfather spent   evenings in the garage,
built a P-40 fighter plane   70% to scale,
flew it himself.   I hold
the day's disturbances   in my hand like stones,
run my fingers over them   until sleep takes them,
gives me other   memories of being
in class again   staring into Old English
manuscripts with students: them noting
the strange writing,   long trains of thorny letters
running margin to margin,   words cutting into words.
Me telling them   someone will come along
and piece out   the units of thought,
add punctuation   and white space,
will find the 4-beat lines,   lay them down in a shape
on the page,   give it a title.

Gianicolo, Rome

> *"Gianicolo certainly deserves a mention as one of the most romantic places to take a date. The panoramic view on Rome's wonders can't be topped."* —www.romabella.com

What must they think: the parents of the children
in the pediatric hospital that faces this scene?
At their edge, a city of earth and myth like mist,
settling low. The houses in terra cotta colors.
Towers where the bells ring out their wordlessness.
Travertine angels along the Tiber, too small to see now;
their fluid stillness, how they used to move them,
a memory. The Castel Sant'Angelo, Il Vittoriano,
the Colosseum.
                      The hospital behind them
rises higher and truer even than the bronze quadriga
placed atop the country's highest court: four muscled horses
and Lady Victory in her chariot reigning over chaos,
beautiful talisman against any injustice below.

Letting Down: 3 Years after the NICU

The garbage truck did not
Come yesterday, on the day
I chose to put out my most

Precious offering—stores of milk
3 years frozen, a 30 gallon
Bag full. Rain fell

As I lay in bed, my milk still waiting
On the street. Today it pools
Below black plastic,

A single ribbon streaming
Across black asphalt toward
Small eddies of oil. The week's

Runoff turns purple, pink, blue as if
Resting on a bubble.
Back inside the house I watch

Furtively like Miriam behind
The bulrushes. From the dark heap
The milk leaks like dread, like hope.

Round Top in March

In the middle of fields of bluebonnets
and wilder flowers, tall, green grasses newly born,
a Frenchman, dealer in antiques, asks me:
Are you lucky?

Am I lucky? I repeat back hesitantly, as if again
in language class. Yes, he says. Are you lucky?
I am his first customer, he says. He says he found a dead rabbit
on his doorstep just this morning. Maybe I have luck, he hopes.

Maybe, I say. I think so.

As I sign the receipt, I muse on the strange superstitions
of other people in faraway lands that I can only
take home in pieces and it makes me feel
more confident about the purchase I have made.

But in the hours it takes to drive back home
and in the days that follow, roadside bluebonnets fading
from pure blue to softer denim, weeds and wildflowers
overtaking them, I think back to the dream of those
fields and the lovely old art sold there and I wonder
how I was not more ready with an answer for the dealer.

I think of a woven Turkish rug, bright
face I designed my room around but left
in Turkey for someone else to buy. How regret retreated

below euphoria, wonder, when I found
the very rug at a small American shop I
happened to walk into, threads of happiness extending
through the tassels.

I think of the weeks, years that passed
before the stolen purse, the job, completely
out of sight returned to view.

Of my son, for whom I bought the beautiful
antique French chest of drawers, who lives freely
and wildly
despite his tragic birth, persistent feeding intolerance
and chronic chylothorax,
all gone now, vanished like the tents and vendors
of the flea market, leaving me alone to think
how lucky I must be.

Symphony

It is late. My husband glides through the water on a final lap. Like an inverted shadow, a plane swims above him, the sky a watery dark. They pull through the world together like a bow and its string, set the world in soft vibration. My younger son, worn tired, climbs into my lap and the stars begin to take their seats above us. Cicadas sing. They wring from the sky a deafening comfort-song, twisting and ringing and singing. The wetness of his hair evaporates, quick as childhood, and his head sleeps to the beating of my heart. I watch the black with my older son, content beside me, and together we play his game of mistaking planes for shooting stars.

Hospital Wall Art
for Atticus

In the catalogue of primary images
this would surely be one: branches
cutting paths through a Greek-blue
sky (though ancients named blue
last, content with Homer's
wine-dark sea). All else for me

in the room—silent-white,
outskirts of the created. I watched it,
tried to read it like tea leaves or tarot cards,
a scene more familiar to me
than my own child's face

upstairs. He would probably be
blind. Would his mind work well
enough to learn the letters of a long name?
I tried to name him, name this.
But before I understood

disability, knew the coolness
meant springtime, not fall, before
I was jealous of the baby
flown in to the children's hospital
with the damaged heart and the healthy

one in the bay next to him with no mother,
before God exploded and I built him back
again years later (lesser, still dear),
in the leafless branches that were
surely clacking together,
all I could see was the letter
A.

Additional Acknowledgments

Many thanks to Baylor University and the department of English, where I have found support for this work, and especially to Dr. Kevin Gardner, our chair. Thanks, also, to Baylor's Institute for Faith and Learning, which has supplied me with a small library of my own and endless friendship.

For making my life richer in so many ways, I also thank the Tankersleys—Kevin, Abby, Sophie, Brazos; the Hogues— Tiffany, Andy, Anna, Caroline; the Ashenfelters—Kasey, Emilee, Phoebe; Leslie Smith, the Hestons, Borderuds, Weavers, Grants, who, along with others at Calvary Baptist Church, Waco, got us through; and my own great big family, the Hancheys, the Fugates, the Fielders, and Mary Poston, soul sister for life. Thanks to Fred and Cathie, Matt and Mary Elizabeth, Sarah, James, Lucy, John, Dorie, Olivia, my grandmother Doris Fugate, my sister Mary, Nate, my brother Brazos, Rachel, Bexar, Bowie, Paul Clark, Michael, Tolya, Andy, and my sister Lauren, always ahead of me. And Mom and Dad—Paula and Mike Fielder—who stayed with us all through the night, and in the day. I love you.

And finally, thanks to the staff members, donors, and volunteers of Cook Children's Hospital in Fort Worth, Texas, and most especially to Dr. Ben Brann and Dr. Meghan Schmidt.

Ginger Hanchey was raised in Dayton, Texas. A graduate of Baylor University and Texas A&M University, her poems have appeared in such publications as *Foundry, Nashville Review, Tar River Poetry,* and *San Pedro River Review.* She lives with her husband and two sons in Waco, Texas and teaches at Baylor.

www.ingramcontent.com/pod-product-compliance
Lightning Source LLC
LaVergne TN
LVHW041602070426
835507LV00011B/1252